SOUL BA

C000116151

A METAPHYSICAL JOURNEY

David L. Oakford

The book cover image is courtesy Freydoon Rassouli created using "Fusion Art" techniques. For more information and to see other creations by Mr. Rassouli at http://www.freydoonrassouli.com/index.html.

Special thanks to Jualt Christos for making the beautiful cover!

Copyediting by Katie Connolly

Contents

Word...

 I'd like to thank those who encouraged me to share this story. This includes my loving family. Thanks you guys. This has helped me and many others. I'd like to thank Kevin Williams, Lilo Kinne, and all of my AOL Chat friends. This is the story I was trying to tell you in the room. I want to thank John Jay Harper (RIP) for helping me write my other books. This book is dedicated to you too. We should look each other up if I go where you are.

For all of you, I have to say that we need to help each of us get along with each other. We need to do this as well as address the issues we've laid on this wonderful planet. Stop polluting the soil and the air. Listen to the experts who know about climate change and help them find ways we can fix this place. Please help them, support them. We need this. We are smart. We can do this.

From what I understand, Gaia is supposed to be our heaven. It was given to us to take care of. We can make it that way. I know we can.

Chapter 1: A Little about Me

Hi! I'm David. I live in Metro Detroit. I'm married and have four wonderful children. To give you an idea about my age, I caught the tail end of the baby boomer generation. I was a kid in the sixties. I have an extremely interesting story to share with you. The story is about an event in my life that occurred in the spring of 1979 when I was nineteen years old.

I went on a guided tour of the universe with a spirit friend who told and showed me why I'm here. "Yeah, right!" you might say. Well, it is OK if you don't choose to believe me. As a matter of fact, I envy those who can choose to not believe this story. I don't have the option to not believe it. I feel I would be overstepping my bounds if I told you what to choose to believe! Besides, I had a tough time accepting the whole experience myself. I admit it all sounds on the "far out" side but I assure you that it happened and I wouldn't be telling it if it were not the truth. My wife will tell you that this isn't something I'm capable of making up.

I've been walking around on this planet for the last several decades trying to figure out what the event really means. I feel that now is the right time for me to share this one major event of my life as completely as I possibly can in hope that whomever reads this story will derive some form of benefit from what I am about to share. However, I do have another motive, which is for me to feel better about it. I feel like I've been holding out on everyone for way too long, thinking that I could keep this all to myself. If this story makes a positive difference in one person's life, then my telling of it will be worth every ounce of effort I expend. Besides, there are people who want to know about it.

I think I've waited for so long to share due to a few personal issues and a need to mature enough to even begin to understand what happened to me, much less explain why it happened. One fear was I would be labeled as crazy. Another reason was that I trained my subconscious mind to feel I was not mature and evolved enough to be able to even give an accurate account of what happened to me. I've also thought that once I got this story out of me fully, my task here on this planet would be finished and I would return to the great white light again. I now feel that I've overcome those fears and, because of that achievement, what happened to me can now be shared.

What happened to me has been described several different ways. Near death experience researcher Kevin Williams received the initial version of my experience in 1998 and called it an extremely profound Near Death Experience. He added the short story version of my experience to his Near Death Experiences and the Afterlife web-site (www.near-death.com). Kevin's site is probably the most popular one for the topic. I wrote and sent the short story version to a friend of mine whose son was dying of cancer in order to assist her and her son to deal with any fears they might harbor about him moving out of the physical realm. The woman (Lilo Kinne, an artist, painter from New York) sent my story to that prominent website that had other folk's stories like mine. This was in '98; the story had 250K hits in its first year, which I believe was pretty viral for the time. I also sent the story as a Christmas present to some of the other interested folks that I had met in the America Online "Metaphysics" chat room. I previously tried to tell the story in the room but it was too long and it always went off topic. Chat rooms...gotta love them. :)

I tended to hang around in the America Online chat-rooms quite often back then. I wanted to share the insights from the story and I liked using the shield of anonymity that a screen name provides to protect myself from possible backlash from me trying to tell it. I could be the true me and feel safe because nobody even had to know my name. I could escape any attacks if needed by simply clicking the X.

I enjoyed quite a few years of extremely interesting chat and met many people who helped me to confirm that what happened to me was indeed very real. They helped me think I might want to share the insights of it all with as many people as possible. I've made countless lasting friendships in the rooms and have been greatly inspired by the love my current friends have given me freely. I am still friends with some of them to this day.

I attempted to tell my childhood friends about what happened to me immediately after I returned to my physical form, and all of them laughed, saying it all was just a bad drug trip. They said to "stop your crazy talk." As young and immature as I was, I was inclined to believe what they said then. I looked like a punk, acted like a punk, and felt like a punk. Who was I to think that I had anything of value to anyone? I eventually met my wife and she made me get rid of those friends first thing. Wives…Thanks honey. I didn't understand about those guys back then. Now I do. I love you forever.

People who believe in some of the more traditional religious doctrines might classify what happened to me as a consort with the devil himself. A psychiatrist would likely classify it as a lucid dream or maybe a form of schizophrenia. A person knowledgeable in the metaphysical arena would call what happened to me a great gift. I could continue to speculate as to what actually happened, but I don't see what more speculation on my part would accomplish. I must say that regardless of how this happened to me, it does make for a very interesting story that is well worth the read.

I prefer not to place any sort of label on the experience. I will tell what happened to me from my own heart and memory. I extend to you an opportunity to decide for yourself what you think the experience was and what you wish to accept from it. Regardless of what labels you may or may not find appropriate, the story is (in my humble opinion) pretty awesome and I feel honored to finally be mature and confident enough to tell it.

Even if you do not feel that the afterlife is real, this story might make for a nice afternoon or so of escape from this business of life. I know it has colored my life in both positive and negative ways and helped me in my growth. I pray it will assist you in your growth. I do care about you deeply and if my sharing will assist you in a positive way, I will feel extremely proud!

I'm not a psychic who can see the future or communicate with the dead. I won't tell you who you were in a past life nor can I tell you when you will meet the love of your life. This story is not something that God himself helped me or told me to write. I am not trying to sell you a lifestyle or a religion or tell you what is wrong or right. I ask and require nothing of you, as I would hope that you would with me.

I was only 19 years old when this happened. I certainly didn't expect or ask for it to happen and was extremely surprised when it did. Since it happened I have denied it, resented it, and even tried really, really hard to forget the entire thing ever happened. I will explain why later. Perhaps I remember because I am supposed to share the story.

I guess I had to grow up quite a bit before I could understand what I saw and felt in my experience. I needed to grow more in order to have enough confidence to feel that people would be interested in this story.

I denied the experience right after it happened because it was an additional entree to add to the already full plate I lugged around from my upbringing. I had enough to deal with already from my childhood alone. The experience was way too heavy for me to take on back then and I felt I wasn't ready to process it. Rather than try to process it, I thought I would be better off forgetting it ever happened. Besides, who would believe me anyway? I was just a ghetto loser who most would think to be the "scum" of the earth. I resented the experience because no matter how I hard I tried to forget, or even understand it, it never went away.

You see, by 1979, I was the proverbial basket case. My self-esteem was nearly nonexistent. I could elaborate here and provide reasons for my condition, but I'll save that for later as well. I will only say that my childhood has been extremely interesting to the therapists I have seen over the years. I've suffered from bipolar disorder, attention deficit disorder, and alcoholism for most of my life, conditions that never completely go away.

I developed an extremely nasty addiction to mood altering substances and alcohol. I made it a point to use those substances as often as possible in an attempt to escape feelings that I just wasn't equipped with to cope with back then. The substances provided a relatively simple, effective, and notoriously reliable means for me to avoid facing these feelings. I could get hammered and then feel good about myself. Drugs and alcohol were an easy solution, and they worked for me a long time.

I eventually progressed to the point where I wanted to get far from the urban neighborhood I grew up in. I wanted to be away from the negative influences that had been the key to me becoming the person I was back then. I think my decision to leave Michigan must have come from a small part of me that was immune to the external influences I had allowed to bring me down, the good in me.

The tiny voice in me grew and matured, increasing in strength and volume despite any efforts on my part to deny it or kill it. My inner self was calling to me, telling me to run away and save myself from the "me" that my mind had been conditioned to tell me I was. I felt this particular voice calling me from my heart. It was the love inside of me, wanting desperately to come out and be free of the prison I kept it in.

I had planned nearly a year in advance to leave Michigan, to go out into the world in an attempt to find out why in the world I had to be on this planet in the first place. I also wanted to see how other people lived. I saw other people in the world that seemed happy, and I wanted to feel that happiness too. I refused to believe I was incapable of it. I believed that if I prepared myself properly, I could find a place that would be better for me. Then I'd have a chance to save myself from myself. I wanted to go out west and ride my bike there. I lost my driver's license for 2 years by being wild with this car I had. I figured I'd get another license and a car when I found my place in another state. I wanted to go out west.

I saved nearly $2000 and prepared myself mentally to sever the remaining ties to my childhood home and family to go out into the world on my own to find my purpose. I felt I needed to find a place that would allow me to clean up my act. I saved the money to make sure I would physically survive long enough to find a place somewhere that might provide me the opportunity to experience the peace I needed to experience. I felt that the peace was somewhere out there, waiting ever so patiently for me to arrive.

I even needed to learn to trust myself! I was ready to go, and I yearned to go. My heart was screaming at me to go, so loudly I couldn't ignore it. It was saying: "RUN!" I even felt in my heart confidence enough to believe that I would accomplish what I was choosing to do, which truly amazed me! Self-confidence was one of the things I had not grown or really felt in my life so far. I was intent on going off and being alone, making my way to wherever my heart would lead me. I was all fired up and ready to go!

The day before I planned to leave I decided I would throw one last party for my friends since I didn't ever plan on seeing them again. Like most young people, my friends were of the utmost importance to me. I felt an obligation to ensure I showed compassion for them. It seemed that even when I screwed up around them, when the next day dawned, I would see them again and the slate would be clean. It was like we were brothers. I could talk to them too. They might not agree with what I had to say to them, but at least they listened to me. They came from similar backgrounds as me and had many of the same problems I had, so they understood me more than anyone else I knew.

The best way I really knew to show my friends how much I cared for them was to give them a good party. Partying was what we always did. Usually at parties we were happy and had a ton of freedom to do whatever we wanted without harming others in the process.

It was at that very party I had what I prefer to call My Experience.

Chapter 2: How This Happened

I fully intended to get really smashed at my final party with my friends. I reasoned that if I got smashed just one more time before I left town, I would be able to look back later and be able to say I was finally done with all of the substances. In the future, I wanted to associate the substances with the environment I was living in at the time and use the memory to prevent myself from returning to it. Besides, it was just one more time...

I was hanging out at one of my friend's homes because his parents were vacationing in Aruba. The group of us observed a tradition of sorts. The tradition was actually an unwritten law requiring members of our group to each offer up the house when our parents left their homes to us alone. We would use the golden opportunity to party. House parties were always the best!

My friend's parents' timing couldn't have been better! The house was one of the larger of the single story brick homes in an area near factories and near the projects. The houses in the neighborhood were small, but this house had a large addition that was fixed up as a party room. There was a pool table, a bar, and an extremely powerful sound system. There were many comfortable chairs and plenty of floor space if someone needed a place to crash. We started partying in the early afternoon.

Toward the evening, the high I had from alcohol and weed was beginning to get boring. I really wanted the night to be special so I decided I would buy something to spice the pot up a bit. I knew who to talk to if I needed any type of illegal drug and arranged for that friend to get me what really could have been anything. It might have been heroin, crystal, crack cocaine or PCP for all I know.

I must pause here and say that I do not endorse substance abuse in any form. What I did with the substances detracted from who I was, as well as delayed the potential of the person I was to become in the future. I also for certain don't recommend that anyone attempt to recreate what happened to me by doing what I did. I was lucky to make it back to here from where I went and I am uncertain how that luck will hold for anyone else. There is no way everyone can win when they gamble! I feel the odds on a gamble like the one I took would be sky high.

My dealer friend came back and gave me a rock of what I thought was some kind of cocaine. I didn't really know anything about the stuff. I thought it was a form of coke that you had to crush up. He told me to wait until he came back before I did anything with it. I decided to go ahead and disregard what he said. I crushed about half of it and snorted it. Then I gave the rest to my friends. The friend that got the rock for me came back, smelled what we were smoking, and asked to see it. When he saw what was left, he asked me where the rest was. I told him I snorted it.

My friend had a very worried look on his face. He told me that I screwed up big time because that stuff was not supposed to be snorted like coke. He reminded me that he had told me to wait. He said I snorted enough to kill me and I would be lucky if I lived through it. Of course, I blew that off completely. I even laughed at him! I felt that I was experienced enough with drugs that I would be OK and told my friend that. Hell, I was an invincible teen. Nothing could hurt me! My friend didn't believe me at all.

Right after that, my friends and I went outside to hang out on the porch and drink some more beers. I could see my parents sitting on their porch from where we were. They were less than fifty yards away. I thought it was pretty funny that there I was, higher than a kite, and they had no idea where I was, what I was doing, or even what I was planning to do! I felt higher than I ever felt in my life and finally thought I felt I was happy at last. I was enjoying myself. It didn't take very long though until I had to sit down because I had trouble standing up. I thought if I sat down that I would be OK and that sitting down under my own power was more attractive than falling down. I sat on the cement porch for a minute. Suddenly, sitting on the cement wasn't working anymore. I started to get a bit scared then because my friend had told me I would probably die. I was starting to get very dizzy, like I was going to lose consciousness.

I lay down on the grass to use the stability of the earth in an effort to maintain my slim hold on reality. I knew I had to do that in order to be able to stay connected enough to ever come back down from this particular high. Being close to the ground was extremely comforting to me, as if I was being held by my mom. The spinning stopped and I faded off into a calm, wonderful sleep. The sleep felt like I was in a cool breeze through a peaceful blackness.

The next thing I remember was riding in my friend's car. My friends were all there with me. I tried to talk to them during the ride but they didn't seem to hear me and I couldn't fully understand what they said. I was only receiving bits and pieces of what they were saying and they couldn't hear what I said at all. We rode around the block and passed directly in front of my childhood home. I remember seeing my parents on the porch and me thinking to duck down in the car. I didn't want my parents to see me like that because then they would know what I didn't want them to know. I remembered that I had done some kind of pretty powerful drug and would get caught for sure if I went home. They would surely punish me if they found out about it.

I thought we drove the way up north in the old blue 74 Chevy Impala 4 door, crossing the Mackinaw Bridge and then turning around to come all the way back to Metro Detroit again. As we traveled, the countryside seemed to me to be in distress. It was like the land was missing something and wasn't quite how it was supposed to be. It wasn't anything I could really see. It was more something that I felt. We rode around my neighborhood past my childhood home again. I saw my parents still sitting on the porch and wondered why they were still there after the long trip I had taken.

As we rode around my neighborhood, I felt a strange attraction to the trees. I could see and feel their strength. I actually saw and felt their roots reaching deep into the ground. I appreciated how they were able to connect with the planet and contribute to it as much or more than what they took from it. I was awed that they seemed to be able to withstand the changes of the seasons and grow in spite of the influences of humans in general.

I saw some little fairy-like looking beings in and around every tree. They looked like the fairies one might see in fairy tale books. They were male, female, young and old and were as diverse in appearance and demeanor as we are. When I looked directly at them, I think they sensed it, then quickly turned away to melt back into the leaves. If I turned my head, or even blinked, they would be gone without a trace.

One of those beings didn't turn away though. He looked me directly in my eyes and smiled a huge, loving smile that hit me directly in the heart. He was about a foot tall, much bigger and older than the others of his kind. He wore very bright colored clothing and from his smile I knew he was positive. I watched him as we drove away. I wondered why he didn't vanish when I looked at him like the others did.

I don't really remember returning to the house and the party. I told my friends about the car ride after the experience and they told me that the only place I went was to the chair they carried me to after I passed out on the porch. My friends didn't even want to talk about that night to me at all and still haven't to this day.

Chapter 3: What Happened To Me?

I thought I woke up in the chair my friends said they put me in. I was in the family room of the house. This was the biggest room in the entire house. I remember there was a bar that actually had liquor in it, a high powered stereo system, and an assortment of nice furniture to crash on. There was shag carpet on the floor so if needs be, someone could crash on the floor. The walls in the room were paneled and there was a door on the northern wall of the room. There were two windows in the room as well. I was in a black Lazy Boy, wondering where my friends were, as well as wondering what my body was doing.

You see, when I woke up, I could feel the organs in my body working, each one separately and in turn in harmony with the others. I could direct my focus on each of my organs and feel their vibration or I could enjoy all of them as one. I could quite plainly hear and feel my heart steadily beating and thoroughly enjoyed feeling my own blood rushing throughout my entire body. Oddly enough, I could actually hear the sounds all of the organs made. They sounded like music. All of them together created a strange, yet familiar and wonderful song of sorts that I cannot even begin to describe. I will say that it was a

18

wonderful harmony that rang true to my heart and the feeling felt right to me.

Eventually, I began to feel my organs begin to shut down. I first felt that my glands were slowing down. As each of them slowed, their part of the beautiful symphony changed. Eventually, when they stopped altogether, their part in the song was gone. Next, went my stomach, liver, and kidneys. Like my glands, all of the rest of my organs slowly stopped, the last of which was my heart. I actually heard the heart stop and felt my blood stop moving. There was an eerie silence then. I didn't know what to think of that at all. I remembered what my friend had told me about doing enough of the drug to kill me, but I was conscious of what I was feeling, so I figured I wasn't dead.

Suddenly, I heard the stereo playing songs from a Doors album, except the volume was way too loud for me. I didn't worry too much then because I thought that if I heard the stereo then I surely couldn't be dead. Needless to say, I felt relieved, but the music was still too loud for me. I had progressed past a point where hearing the song my body had been playing was overridden by Jim Morrison. I did enjoy loud rock music then, and still do, so at that moment I wondered why all of a sudden the music bothered me. At that point, the music began to become very annoying, but it wasn't the same as hearing my body in the amplified manner I had been hearing it. The songs were definitely not the same.

I couldn't see my friends anywhere. I could see in all the rooms of the house at the same time just by thinking about them. The ability seemed totally natural to me and I didn't question it at all. I found the entire house to be empty. All there was in the house was me and the music. Since I didn't see any friends, I got up and tried to turn the music down but couldn't. I couldn't find the volume control. I couldn't find the plug either. No matter what I did, the music kept playing louder and louder. I knew that stereo well too. I had a serious problem with the noise. It was clawing at me and I couldn't figure out why or how I could adjust the volume or just turn the thing off.

I called out for my friends and nobody came. I tried to unplug the stereo again but that still didn't work. I found the cord but I couldn't grab it no matter how many times I tried. The stereo just kept on playing songs from a Doors tape. The sound in general rattled my very being. It just grew louder and louder and I couldn't stop it. I had no sense of touch whatsoever. I thought it must be just the effects of the drugs and it would wear off over time. I felt alive, but I still definitely needed to do something about the noise that was growing increasingly louder every second. I became afraid because what I knew to do in this type of situation had no effect.

I ran all over the house calling for my friends, shrieking that the music was too loud. I was not heard. I didn't see them around anyway. I resorted to begging for the music to be turned down. I tried to go outside to escape the noise but since I couldn't feel the doorknob, I couldn't turn it. I saw the daylight outside through the window but couldn't get out there.

I looked out the window. Everything outside looked very odd to me. Everything was more detailed than normal. I saw colors around things I could not see before and didn't know what they were. I really wanted to go out there and explore the world, but couldn't figure out how I could make that happen. I was curious. Opening doors and windows and turning down the volume all were beyond my capabilities at that point.

I ended up hiding in the bathroom in an unsuccessful attempt to escape the noise. I tried to pee but couldn't grab it. I tried to wash my face but couldn't work the faucet. Like the stereo, the door, and everything else, I couldn't feel any of them. I couldn't even pick up a towel so I could use it to muffle the music that seemed to be crawling toward me through the bottom of the door!

I happened to look in the mirror and discovered that I couldn't see myself. That put me over the edge right then and there. I started to panic. I could not see me, feel me, or touch me or anything else. I ran around the house crying like a baby and calling for my friends to help me, but nobody answered me and nobody came to help. Running was becoming harder to do too. Have you ever run in a dream and not gotten anywhere? That is exactly what trying to move around felt like to me.

I finally found my way back into the family room and saw my body sitting in the chair. It looked like I was sleeping. I wondered how I could be looking at myself. I was kind of glad to see me there, but wondered then how I could be in two places at once. I became even more scared then because I saw me from outside of me from all different angles, except from the inside angle I was used to seeing from. All I had to do was think of the angle I wanted and immediately my view changed to the one I thought of, except that inside one. I didn't like how I looked in any of the angles. I looked ugly and I could tell there was something missing. I had this feeling that what was missing was me that was looking at my body. I still felt alive though.

I was alone too. I was confused and terrified. I frantically attempted to get back into my body by sitting on it a few times but couldn't connect to it. My body seemed every bit as untouchable as everything else I tried touching. I couldn't touch the ground either. I was floating. I rose up slowly into a spot just above and to the left of my body and kind of just hung there for a bit. It became even harder to move. I screamed out for help again and nobody came. Somehow I managed to get to the door again, but like before, I still couldn't touch the doorknob. I didn't know what to do. All of the things I thought I should do, I couldn't do because my physical self would not accept the commands I gave it. I didn't understand what was happening to me at all and had run out of ideas of what to do about it.

I went back near my body and thought to ask God to help me. I figured that lots of people pray to something, maybe it would work for me too. I didn't believe in God then, but I was kind of angry at him because of the difficult life I was experiencing. I reasoned that if God were really the omnipotent and omniscient being the Christian religions taught me he was, he would not have allowed me to experience the pain and hardship I had experienced throughout my life. I felt that since that God allowed me to experience the suffering I must have done something to deserve it. After all, the churches said that not following the 10 Commandments meant damnation and punishment eternal. I thought maybe since I didn't live my life perfectly according to what the religions taught me I was experiencing punishment for it through my suffering.

I used to pray to God quite a bit as a child because I knew in my heart that there was such a being and that was well before I was taught of him by the churches. The Gods the churches taught me and the God I knew in my heart were very different. When I prayed for keeps, I prayed to the God of my heart, not the ones the churches sought to make me aware of. It's hard for me to explain really. I think the difference between the two is that the God that the churches taught me was a God who punishes while the God of my heart is loving and kind and does not punish. He creates positive things. The God of my heart would accept me regardless of what I had ever done and help me try to fix it. The God of the churches seemed to me to be conditional with his love, even to the point that he would choose to give up on his creations and destroy them or send them to what they call hell. I didn't believe in the God of the churches because I didn't feel God to be unable to love without condition.

Actually, the more deeply I thought about it, I knew the God of my heart was the only friend I had that I could talk to and trust he would listen. I was certain he would help me regardless of anything I have ever done, if I approached him with the feelings of my heart. I thought that if there ever was a time I needed that God, it was now! I thought: "God, my friend, I really need some help here and I know that if anyone can help me, it would be you. Will you please help me? I think I might have seriously messed up this time." I wasn't disappointed with the result of my plea for help.

Chapter 4: The Light Being

For some reason, I glanced over to the door leading to the outside and saw this extremely beautiful being just over there, floating exactly the same way I was floating. His feet didn't touch the floor either. They just blended in to thin air, like my own feet did. He had some sort of robe on that was light in color, a sort of off-white. His hair was a light brown, very curly, somewhat long, and it shimmered around him as he floated. His face was very pleasant to see. He looked female, male and young like me. His gender was really inconclusive. If I perceived him to be male, he appeared to seem more male in appearance. If I chose to perceive him to be female, he appeared to be more female. From either point of view there was no way for me to decide this thing's sex at all. At that point, gender wasn't all that important to me anyway. The being was here when nobody else was there. He was all I had at the moment. The Doors began to fade away.

He was about my size. There was a shimmering glow about him too. The glow was green close to him, then blue, then pure white in the upper areas. He looked so awesome! He spoke to me. He said, "I am here to help you" but when he spoke his mouth didn't move. I didn't actually hear him speak. I felt what he was saying and there was no doubt in my mind that he was talking directly to me.

As I looked at this beautiful being and felt it speaking to me, my fears faded away. The music by then had faded completely away. I actually felt peace and comfort like I never felt before. I thought that maybe this was the peace I was searching for my entire life. This feeling of peace started to become strangely familiar to me, like I had felt it before but not in this life. I thought that maybe this being was God. He knew I thought that, smiled an affectionate smile, and said, "No, I am not God." I was amazed he knew what I was thinking and figured that this is how we were going to communicate.

This wonderful being then called me by a name I really wish I would remember. I told him he must have the wrong guy and that the name he used for me wasn't my name. He said I had just forgotten who I am.

This being told me his name, but I don't remember it and I'll explain why later. For now I'll call him Bob, just to give him a name. He told me that he had always been with me and told me that he knew that I had a very hard life and that he would help me understand why that was so, if I really wanted to know. He told me he would help me remember who I really am. He said he would understand if I didn't believe him and then offered to prove to me that he knew everything about me.

Bob told me things that I did when I was a child that proved to me that he was always with me. He told me about things I had only thought about and never expressed to anyone. Basically, he told me my deepest and darkest secrets. He provided some examples of what caused me to become so depressed and angry so early in my life. He showed me why I became the way I am. He told me what I thought of and how I felt when I when I went to bed at the ages of two and three. He knew all of my personal stuff, for sure.

He then offered that I was someone from history whose name I did recognize at the time and that I had returned to physical form this time to complete what I had started back then. He said that he would help me to remember who I am. Bob said that "David Oakford" was my name in this physical existence only. He explained that I am someone else in spirit and that I would eventually combine both David and my spirit self with each other in a nice harmonic balance. I would eventually combine of the best qualities of both of those aspects of myself in this lifetime if I should choose to apply myself in a manner that would create the harmony within me. He said it was entirely my free choice and my task and if I chose not to apply myself in that manner it would be OK. There would be consequences either way.

He said that I was one of the very first of my kind on the planet. I carry a special part in me that would help populate the planet with people who would help their fellow humans and the planet to restore their harmony with the universe. I didn't fully agree that this planet needs something or someone to help it along. I feel the special part that he mentioned is either my DNA or the love which lives in my heart and my DNA.

I liked talking telepathically. His language was very eloquent and sometimes difficult to understand; however, he understood me perfectly and I could understand enough of the main points he made. The expression on his face was a happy one all the time and when he spoke to me he did so in a manner that was positive, assertive, and nurturing in tone. He did not criticize me or my family at all. I don't remember anything he said which I could possibly construe as negative in nature.

I remembered the church talking about Satan and hell. They say hell is a place that is essentially a lake of fire and Satan can disguise himself in order to deceive you into going there. Bob told me that hell and Satan are none of my concern. He said I was a positive light being and I should look at other entities by examining their intent. If their intent benefits only them or is negative toward others, I might not want to interact with them. Bob was always positive. I could see his intent was positive.

He told me I could travel with him to anywhere I wanted to go and he would show me how to do it if I wanted him to. He said if I felt the need to come back at any time to see my body at any time, I could do that. I was skeptical. I guess he felt my concern about my body and me separating. He explained that my body would be fine because I had a spiritual cord connected to it somehow and would stay connected until I made my own free choice to disconnect myself from it.

I was faced with deciding where I wanted to go. For sure, I wanted to leave that house and my childhood neighborhood, but I had difficulty deciding where I wanted to go. Although I somewhat trusted this being, I still doubted whether what he was telling me was true. Eventually I figured that since this being was with me, I chose to give him the benefit of that doubt. After all, he came as a result of me asking the God of my heart to help me and I felt it might not be a good idea to question what I was given too much. What else did I have to do anyway?

I thought that it might be fun to see the Seven Wonders of the World. I thought that I might have chosen something more profound given the wide-ranging option I was given, but the Seven Wonders were what I thought of first and in retrospect, I feel I chose as wisely as I possibly could at the time.

Bob laughed and then proceeded to explain to me that there are different types of wonders: natural and ones built by humans. Many of them have been destroyed. He said he would show me two, Egypt and the Southwest USA. I had already seen and felt the Grand Canyon as a boy but he said if I still wanted to go to there again it would be fine. See Egypt and the Grand Canyon? Hell yes! I was going to go!

He told me that all I had to do was trust him, think about where I wanted to go, and we would go. I thought about the pyramids, trusted my guide and we arrived in Egypt in an instant! It was like we got there in merely the scant time it takes to think a thought!

Chapter 5: Traveling the Planes of Existence

I don't know why I chose the pyramids, but they were my first thought so I went with it. I saw the pyramids as they were in 1979 as well as how they were in the ancient times. When I saw them, I saw them from each point of view separately, and then I saw spirit people from both eras coexisting together. I asked how it could be that the past and present could be together as one and was told that the life on the planet worked that way in order to be in harmony with itself. It's just how it is. What I was seeing were the energies of different dimensions and what I was shown was how they interact.

I saw how the choices of the past help determine the options for the choices of the present. I also saw how the choices made in the present potentially affect what will occur in the future. The beings I saw from the past would make their choices and the beings in the present would see the options for their choices based on what the beings in the past had chosen.

I understood that I was once a part of the past that I was seeing and felt that my existence as a human this time was directly related directly to something I had done in that particular past life. I played the role of a bad guy and did something that killed a bunch of people. I don't remember exactly what that was and I'll explain why later as well.

My current life's mission was somehow related to the decision I made then. My guess is this time that I'm a good guy and need to be really good to right the wrongs I am responsible for.

The past and current eras rivaled each other in beauty and from the point of view I had then, the harmony of the choices I observed made perfect sense to me. The pyramids were white and the city there was flourishing in the ancient view. The other view was a modern city.

While we were there, I was told some things about the pyramids and Egypt I do not fully remember now. I do not remember the specifics but the subject pertained to the energy of the planet and the role the pyramids have played and still can potentially play in it. There were also facts given about the function of the pyramids and an explanation of why as well as how they were built.

I really do wish I could remember the specifics of what he explained while we were there because I do know they were highly significant and concerned mankind's future. I think that I might not remember the specifics of this because I might not yet be ready to remember, humanity is not yet ready for me to share them, or that particular memory was taken away somehow.

I had seen and experienced all that I could in Egypt. My friend explained to me the why and how of things there which I previously had no idea even existed and wouldn't and couldn't possibly have thought of myself. After Bob had enlightened the soul "me" of those things, I saw no reason to stay there. Besides, I still could pick wherever I wanted to go and I wanted to take full advantage of that. I felt that if there was so much for me to learn from going to but one tiny place on the planet, there was no limit as to what I could see and learn now.

We left Egypt and proceeded toward the southwest United States. We flew there slowly because I wanted to see the sights along the way. I wanted to see this entire planet with the vision I had then. On the way I saw the countries of the Far East and the Pacific Ocean. As we flew I could see the energies of the countries we passed. I saw that if the area we were near had large cities, the energy was less in intensity from a natural standpoint than it was in the undeveloped areas.

I felt and saw great energies as we flew above the Pacific Ocean as well. I was told that the oceans were where the energies of the planet were the most natural in essence. There were only a few select places on the land with energy that rivaled that in the oceans. The reason given for that was that humans have not yet affected the energies in those places as they have on the rest of the landmasses. These were very special places, and there were not many of them. They had to do with the planet's purest energies.

It seemed to me that the choices made by humans had a direct correlation with the energies of entire planet. If humans lived in an area, the energy there was definitely not the same as the natural areas.

The energies I saw in the cities of eastern countries like India, Tibet, the Middle East and Africa were higher in level than those I eventually saw in the United States. The reason given was that groups of people in those countries were more in tune with the energies of the planet and the universe than groups in the United States. It seemed that the more the development, the more negative energy. The energies of the United States were definitely different. Night was falling in the southwest US when we arrived in the area. I could see clearly the energies emanating from everything I could see, especially the plant and animal life. In keeping with everything I had seen thus far, the energy was strongest in the areas of the land that had the least amount of humans. It was cool to see the lights from the cities. I felt a strange attraction to the moon too. It looked even prettier than it normally does, if that's possible.

I was shown souls who had higher energy levels and some of them actually talked to the being I was with. Those entities were the higher level beings that worked in the cities and at the special energy places of the world. Some of them were just like my friend and others were more like me. The ones like him were very high in vibration and the ones like me were lower in vibration, but I could see that it was because they were still attached to their physical bodies in the same manner as I was. The difference between those who had a physical body and those who didn't was readily apparent due to the intensity of their vibration. Physical bodies had less energy; souls in spirit have more.

During the whole time the being and I spent on the planet Earth, I also saw dark souls. The dark souls were earthbound spirits who refuse to go to the Light. The Light is a sort of porthole that souls can go to if they choose, but for them to choose it, they would have to acknowledge it was there and make a conscious decision within themselves to go to it. If they can't or won't do it, they remain on the earth and wander aimlessly or stay stranded wherever they are. Over time, they forget everything and the opportunity to go to the Light fades for them. I myself saw no Light.

Yes, ghosts do exist. They are all around us. I have seen them.

The dark souls usually prey on the energies of humans still in human form and try to use those souls to prevent the evolution of spirit or to satisfy their own desires. If the dark souls understand what the light is all about, they might make a conscious decision not to go to the light. They sometimes attempt to influence other wayward souls and humans who do not understand the light and keep them from it too.

I understood I was and would always be protected from these dark ones as long as I chose to focus on the love in me. I was told that I eventually I could assist the dark souls to the Light if I were to show myself to be the essence of the Light. I understood that essence to be Love. The dark ones didn't even try to affect either Bob or me. In fact, they gave us nasty looks and went away. Their energies were dark and dull colors like browns and blacks and reds.

I was thankful that I had Bob to teach me about these things. I was told I would know these dark ones when I see them and I could alert them to the fact that they can go to the Light just by being loving and kind to them without placing conditions on the love that I send to them.

I could see energy around the humans too, all different levels and colors. My light being explained the human energy to me. He said that the energy coming from humans is what spirits like him utilize to evaluate their spiritual condition and intent. Humans produce and manipulate their energy through their interactions with the environment around them as well as their intent. This energy is a tool that assists spirit to evaluate the spiritual condition of the souls that had left their human bodies and then determine the best way to help them to the Light.

My light being said the more brilliant the color, the higher the vibration is. He said that seeing the "aura" around a spirit is very useful in determining how much help a particular spirit needs to work on his development. He said the beings of higher vibration know where to go and what to do to help humans and earthbound souls so they may advance themselves if they so choose. He told me that all souls have this energy; this is why I could see it on every human I saw. The energy of the aura of a human is what links it to the planet. Its absence from the body results in what we humans think to be death.

He said that I was of the same energy type as he is but my vibration is lower when I inhabit human form and that in time my energy would raise to match his intensity provided I chose to take the initiative to consciously evolve my soul in a positive way. He told me that to evolve my soul I would need to choose to practice love and kindness to all things and learn to live in harmony with the planet and my human body. It seemed simple enough and I thought I should try. I never really tried to do it before.

He talked some more about of the dark souls who would attempt to influence my evolution and said that I would know them by gauging their intent as well. If what they said or did detracted from the harmony of the planet or the universe in any way, they would be harnessing the negative spectrum of the energy of the universe. If their intent were only for the good of them or negative in nature, those are good guidelines to use if I should believe what they might try to tell me. He said if I wished to choose the negative type of intent I was free to do so, but again by universal law I would have to face the effects of what I choose. Basically I have free will that allows me to choose my own destiny

The negative energy was originally meant to be a tool to enhance the evolution of souls, but over time humans have overused and abused that gift.

Positive and negative energies properly balanced were the intent of the original makeup of the energies. The concept of this worked well on the planet until human free will choices tipped the scales on the equation.

He told me that there is much to this planet that spirits can see which humans do not see with their eyes because their vibrations are so low. He showed me life in the trees and inside the earth that I could see as a spirit but could not see in my human form. I remembered the beings I saw in the beginning of my experience and asked him if they were part of the life he was speaking of. He told me that I was correct in my thinking.

He explained that those beings of higher vibration do live on Earth but they are not human - they are part of Earth itself. He explained these beings were the caretakers of physical life of the planet. Bob said that these beings take care of what we call nature. They take care of the plant life, the mineral life, and the waterborne life. These plant spirits work together to ensure that all aspects of nature are protected and remain healthy. While the planet evolves, these ethereal beings are the physical caretakers of the balance and essence of nature.

Bob explained to me that the planet that we call Earth really has a proper name in the universe, just as he and I do. He told me the Earth is really called "Gaia." He said Gaia has its own energy and that Gaia is really a true living being. She is one of the more significant entities of the universe. She is a beautiful lady of abundance! I asked if her energy could be seen like the energies I had been seeing and he said that we have to move away from Gaia a bit to see and appreciate her completely.

He said humans are the ones who manipulate Gaia's energy through their choices. He said if humans choose to live in harmony with the energy on Gaia, it is good for Gaia and enhances Gaia's energy. He said if humans abuse Gaia by not observing the harmonic balance of nature, this hurts Gaia because it alters Gaia's true energy structure in negative ways and cause serious damage to it.

I was given an example of how humans have deforested the planet and reduced the energy available faster than it could be replenish itself through the process of nature. What I saw were the energies of the land of the Pacific Northwest. The contrast between the areas where the trees were removed and where they remained was clearly evident to me. My friend explained to me Gaia was very strong indeed, but has been weakened considerably since humans have chosen to use resources like trees and minerals in

41

a manner that is inconsistent with the laws of the universe. The idea is to use the resources as Gaia produces them and leave to Gaia what she needs to continue to produce. Once the base energy structure is altered on Gaia, this causes Gaia to alter the harmony in the rest of universe as well.

All of that made sense to me because I knew that I in essence was doing the same thing to my own body when I abused substances. Not only was I hurting me, I was hurting everyone else as well through my own choices. When using substances I was altering the energies I emitted. That same principle applied to my thoughts. If I was fearful or angry, the energies I put out carried to whatever was around me and bred more of the same energy dependent on the subsequent choices made by those who my energy affected.

I asked Bob if we could go into space and see Gaia's energy and he said yes. He said there were no limits on where we could go. I concentrated my thought, trusted, and we then went into what is known as space. I didn't hesitate at all!

Away from this planet, I could see Gaia all at once. It was so beautiful. I could see the aura around Gaia and it wasn't the atmosphere - it was bigger. That aura affected me greatly. The effect on me was like seeing the birth of my children! It was mostly blue, surrounded with a lot of bright white, but it was the most brilliant blue I have yet to see. It would have been still more beautiful were it not for the destruction humans have dealt since they came to Gaia.

I felt a deep love for this beautiful place. I could hear the lady move and was told the sound was the energy flowing in and out of her. It reminded me of the song I heard my body playing when I first remember being in the chair in the house. Of course, it was much grander in scale.

My special being told me that Gaia is most unique because it is designed for humans to live on forever. It was created for spirit to play, learn, and grow. He said the balance of nature on Gaia is what allows spirit to be in human form. If that human form lives in harmony with nature, it has more fun, learns more, and grows more than if it chose to not observe the harmonic balance.

The nature also exists on Gaia to compensate for the decreased vibration required for a human to maintain a physical presence. Nature was created for spirits so they could adapt enough to adjust and be in the physical human body while still having access to energies of the universe and each other which will help both. Bob explained that humans and the planet were designed by the creator to live on Gaia for eternity.

He said that "dying" is a human-created Earth term that means little in the world of spirit. The reason humans die is partly because they have fallen away from the balance of nature and are thus inevitably affected by what they choose to create that violates the natural laws of the universe. The other part is how souls evolve. He said that humans have fallen away from living in balance with nature and each other and because of that have shortened the time available for them to be in a physical form like I was.

That discussion made me wonder how humans came to be on Gaia in the first place. My special friend told me that I was first given my gift of an existence on Gaia around the time when Gaia first had humans on it. I asked him what Gaia was like then and all of a sudden I was on Gaia again. I was in a tropical type area. Everything was so perfect and warm and felt so right. I remember waking up hungry, then standing up and walking, going to explore. I was surrounded by only nature and awesome, positive energies.

No sooner than I felt that I wanted to stay there forever I was back in space again and continuing my journey. Bob explained some things about where I went that time. I wish I could remember the details about what he told me, and I suppose I will remember when I am ready. I think I may have gotten a bit too inquisitive at that point! I will say that I believe that I was given either a glimpse of ancient past, or maybe a feeling of what the Gaia of the future may feel like. Either way, it was very inspiring to me and I would not mind feeling that feeling again sometime!

He said again that humans must remember about the harmonic balance if they want to survive as a race and live eternally on Gaia. I asked if that meant that we would eventually transcend death and become what we term as immortal in the way he said was originally intended for us. I was given "no" as an answer. Bob said no, we are already immortal because we have souls that never die. He said it was still possible for humans to learn about this harmony and that it is the next overall goal that the humans on Gaia will eventually attain. How long it would take depends on the choices humans make as individuals, and as a whole. It's all up to us.

I was told that humans would eventually realize they must restore the harmony but great damage will be inflicted before humans fully realize what they have been doing to Gaia and choose to work to reverse it. The damage inflicted will be to humans, as well as to Gaia itself.

The cause and effect of the individual choices made by each human in a collective sense is what will determine the outcome. I was told that I could contribute to the eventual restoration of the harmony by ensuring that my thought, word, and deed are designed by my intent to provide a positive outcome for everyone.

All of what Bob said made sense to me. I could see how my thoughts matter to the collective scheme of things. As I watched Gaia, I reflected on what I was feeling, hearing and seeing. As I thought about what I was being shown, I thought I'd ask about the other parts of the universe that my thoughts and deeds affected.

I looked toward the moon, thought about it, and suddenly we were there. I saw very little of the energies from on Gaia there and I asked why the moon was so different. He joked that one of the moon's functions is to provide a rest stop for travelers like us! However, the moon's main function is to serve Gaia by helping Gaia to stay aligned with the rest of the universe. The moon assists Gaia to harness the energies in the universe that enables it to support itself and produce its unique nature. When Gaia produces nature, it returns the energies it used from the

46

universe. The moon is a type of governor for the energies. It keeps Gaia from being overwhelmed by them. It also serves as a type of conduit that services the transference of energy from Gaia to the rest of the universe.

Of course, those made me think of all of the other planets in our solar system. I wondered about the stars too. If Gaia and the moon were so connected, where would the other planets and stars fit into all of this? No sooner than I thought of those things, we were traveling toward the other planets and stars at a totally immeasurable speed.

Chapter 6: Meeting One Great Master

We traveled closely past all of the planets in our solar system on our way to a star that I chose randomly. When we neared each planet we slowed and I could hear their energies just like when we were near Gaia. Each one sang a song that sounded differently than the other. I saw the auras around each one of them as well. All were beautiful in their own right.

I saw spirit on every one of those planets too. Bob told me that each planet is a place for spirit to live, learn, and thus evolve. I saw great cities on each and every one of those planets. I wondered how there could be cities there and why humans not seem to know of them. Bob explained that many facets of life in the universe cannot readily be seen by humans because those facets were all of higher vibration. Bob said that most spirits of physical human form have yet to attain the higher level of vibration that is required to be able to see the dimensions comprising the higher levels of the energies of the universe.

I understood that each planet has a theme for learning and that any one of them can be chosen by a soul when we are between physical lives. He said we practice on the other planets to get ready to live on Gaia. Bob said Gaia is the ultimate experience for a soul. It is ultimate because our souls evolve faster there than anywhere else and that we apply what we learn on the other planets when we come to Gaia. We are able to be physical here. I gathered that we need some lessons that are difficult to learn without having a physical form.

I learned that we pick a physical life on Gaia. Bob told me that I picked the parents I was born to so that they could help me learn what I needed to grow enough to come back and do spirit work on Gaia after I attain a certain level of growth. I was to help them complete their paths. He said I was being told all of these things so that I could help souls come together and return Gaia to harmony.

We arrived at the star. The star looked like it was sucking the energies of rest of the universe into itself, which I didn't expect. We were close to it, but we weren't close enough that we would be sucked in. If I had to describe this thing, I would compare it to a whirlpool, a tornado, or perhaps a tunnel of some sort. It spun like a spiral, and had a distinct center to it that was very calm. I wondered what made it and what it was for. I thought maybe God did it because a lot of folks on Gaia say so.

I could see, hear, and feel that there was something wonderful on the other side of it too. I wanted to go through it but Bob said I'm not ready yet and it would be dangerous. He said he can't go there yet either. Maybe someday we can. Maybe there are other universes and this is a portal to them.

Bob explained a few things to me about God. Some of what he said I remember and some I don't. What I don't remember had to do with the size and physical structure of the universe. I do remember he said that God is not physically seen for he is everything. He is the energy. He can go beyond the portal I was seeing to seek assistance of other entities of his level. The portal might have been a door to another universe that I wondered how these places have their own creators.

He told me that God loves the lady Gaia and the rest of this universe deeply, as much as a man would love and help their soul group on Gaia. I was told God is a representative of this universe and goes into and out of this portal to get the assistance he needs from other entities like himself to help him to maintain his universe.

Bob talked about Jesus too. He told me Jesus was one master who made an agreement with God to come to Gaia to be an example for humans on how to act toward each other and find their way back to the path of harmony with each other as well as with Gaia. I was told that Jesus is but one of the masters entrusted by God to ensure that souls evolve. He said that Jesus is of the highest vibration compared to any other spirit. He said that God holds the Master Jesus in high favor because he is perhaps the best, a widely known example on Gaia of what humans can attain on Gaia because he attained his mastery the same way that we can if we choose to work toward it!

I then got to see the master I felt to be Jesus. He joined us and at first looked similar to how the churches taught me he looked. I didn't see him like that for very long at all though because he changed into his light. Jesus's light was the purest I have ever seen. Totally white. There was no need for words. There were only love-like feelings sweeping over me that I cannot even begin to describe.

I was told by this master entity that loving one another is what souls need to do in order for peace and harmony to become fully felt on Gaia. He said just that, and then he left.

Bob told me there is an established hierarchy in the universe dedicated to preserving harmony. I do not remember the specifics of that. I was told of a structure of spirit beings that was carefully planned and is extremely important to the inner workings of all that there is. These include angels and guides and ethereal beings that take care of Gaia. I was told that physical humans are one of the most important and vital parts of this thing called the harmonic balance. The free will we have is the part of our souls that allows us to give positive service to the universe, if we decide to do that. On the other side of this, the free will can also be used for negative purposes.

After Bob explained those things to me, I was able to see our whole solar system all at once in full color and sound. The planets were all in a line and I could see all of them to the sun. I could hear and feel the song they sang together. I felt so very blessed and extremely important. I felt like I was given this really awesome gift but I didn't really understand why. There I was, a negative person who went out my way to inflict pain on other souls, yet I wasn't even asked about what I had done with my life. In fact, I was given the honor of being given answers to questions that I'm sure many people wonder about all of their lives.

I thanked Bob for explaining and showing me what he did. He told me that there was more for him to show me if I was ready to experience it. I told him I was ready. I didn't know why I was chosen for any of this but I wasn't about to question why. It just seemed like a minor detail to me then.

I let Bob decide where to go next. He said there was somewhere we needed to go. I didn't have any ideas on where to go other than going into the star and since I couldn't do that yet I felt that it might be best to let Bob decide where we were to go. It seemed he had an idea. I knew I wanted to learn as much as possible from him and I felt he knew what I needed to learn. I completely trusted him. Any doubts I had harbored about this whole experience vanished. We moved away from the star.

Chapter 7: The Spirit City

We started to head back toward Lady Gaia. I thought we were going back to Gaia, but we went to a place that seemed to be in her shadow. We were close, close enough that we could see Gaia from there, aura and all. I wondered how these places have not been seen by someone before. It looked like there were spirits going to and from Gaia. They left trails that faded away, sort of like the contrails from the planes we see in our skies.

It was a great city that seemed to be in the clouds. The place seemed like it was another planet but it wasn't, or maybe it was another dimension.

There were these beautiful white buildings as far as I could see. All of them had wood frames with plants merging themselves to framing. I saw spirits living there all that had vibration but no real physical human bodies as I knew them on Gaia. They were just like me, light. These inhabitants went to and from the buildings, going to work and going to play. They were as diverse as we humans are. I saw a place where spirits went to get what I think to be water. There were no vehicles there at all. Spirits there seemed to get around the same way my being and I got around and that was by flying. It was an extremely busy place. I wondered what it is they actually do there.

The city had no boundaries that I could see. This place was full of life of every kind. There was nature there, many pure plants, trees, and water just like on Gaia but more pure. Nature there was absolutely perfect. It was untainted by human manipulation. I felt an extremely strong positive vibration there. The place was so very similar to Gaia. All that was missing were the problems and negativity I felt on Gaia. I felt that this was what is called heaven in Earth terms. Guess what? I could touch things there too!

I saw spirits going to and from Gaia and the city. I could tell the development of the spirits going to and from by feeling the energy they put out. I could see that animal souls came to and from Earth just like humans do, and I could feel their feelings as well.

I could see many souls leave Gaia with guides and could see souls returning to Gaia with and without guides. My guide told me that some of the spirits passing to and fro were the ones he mentioned earlier that were doing the work with humans on Gaia. I could distinguish between the types of spirits that were doing the work from the spirits that were coming to the great city to become replenished and eventually go back to Gaia to experience more and further evolve. I could feel the emotions of the souls coming back for replenishment. I could feel that some of them were sad, beaten, and scared, much like I felt before my being came to me. I felt many others that were returning to this wonderful home full of love and light and positive energy.

My guide took me into one of the larger buildings. Inside I saw many spirits working. They were doing things similar to jobs on Gaia. I saw a place where there were people who were working with things ranging from simple paint and paper to things that I could not recognize. There were also classrooms where souls were learning all about Gaia. It seemed like what the spirits were doing were more along the lines of what we would consider art here on Earth. It also seemed to me that what was going on in this place was all about Gaia and firmly connected to her.

When we walked by the spirits that were working, they all looked at me. I think they were checking me out because of the being I was with. We went up some stairs and I saw a few spirits that knew me and I recognized them from somewhere. They greeted me and asked me how I was doing on Gaia and why I was here. They seemed happy to see me and each gave me advice which unfortunately, I do not remember. I thought I was going to be given a job like them, but my guide knew I thought that and told me that there was something I needed to do first. He said I wasn't quite ready.

I was ecstatic! I thought I was in heaven despite everything I had done during my life on Gaia. I was experiencing what most people only dream about. The love I felt there was the same love I felt when I saw the light of the great master Jesus. I think the place I had wanted to search for on Gaia was really the same place I was in then. I was searching on Gaia for the feeling I was feeling that very moment. I had found the feeling that I spent my whole life searching for. I was truly happy. I was home and I knew it. I was fully ready to stay in this place and perform any task I was assigned to do. I wondered a little that maybe there was some sort of catch involved here.

My guide then took me to another building that seemed more special than the rest. It was much bigger than the other buildings. The greenest foliage I have ever seen was growing on it, decorating it like a shrine. Many spirits came and left from this place. We went inside and saw on one side a set of double doors that glowed with life. On the other side was a long corridor that led to a large hall. Along the corridor were rooms. Bob told me that this hall was where souls' records are kept. The entire inside of the building was decorated with a wood paneling that the being told me was a glowing, "living" wood from the trees that grew at this wonderful place.

He led me to some big double doors and told me to wait on this bench made of the same glowing wood while he went in through the double doors. As I sat on the bench, I started to remember things about the life I had in Egypt. I was a young boy living alone on the streets. I had told a priest a secret I'd overheard in my travels. I almost became aware of what that secret was but I got interrupted.

My guide came out of the room. He suggested that I go into the room. He said he would wait for me when I came out and told me to not worry. He did caution me to ensure that I was truthful with the beings in the room in the event that they asked me questions. He said they were not judges; rather they were the ones who evaluated a soul's development based on a soul's recorded history. The records were the same ones stored in the same building.

He told me to remember who I was and to refrain from fear. I knew I had to leave this being sooner or later but I was glad that he would wait for me. I was a bit scared to leave him, but I felt protected and knew in my heart that I would be protected here.

I gathered myself together, grasped one of the golden knobs, and walked through those doors.

Chapter 8: The Council

I saw a group of several spirits seated at a round table. The table was made of the glowing wood and was perfect in every way. There was a spot at the table for me. The spirits around this table had the highest vibration I had seen so far with the exception of the master Jesus.

I looked at these beings and recognized them immediately and a chill surrounded me. I knew that these beings were serious in nature because of the energies that swept over me as I walked into the room. I don't know where I recognized them from, but they all were familiar. They just looked at me. I knew I had been to that very room before and I knew that this place was a serious business room. These beings each had their own specialty. It was almost like they each had some aspect of me that they were responsible for and know everything about. I felt a deep sense of respect for them and even feared them because of their obvious status. I was very afraid of one of them more than the others. I remembered he was the one I dealt with concerning the Egypt thing.

All of a sudden, I saw my parents on Earth before I was born. I saw how those being together all came about and watched my brother and sister join them before me. I saw my parents' positive and negative sides and evaluated them according to what I knew I needed to do on Gaia. The beings asked me how and why I picked these particular parents and asked me to tell them. They said I knew how and why I picked them and asked me to tell them why. I do not know where it came from but I did tell them how and why and they agreed with me. I picked them to help them on their paths as well as to achieve my learning. We needed each other. I agreed with their souls and the universe to help them and I did it before they even came to Gaia.

I saw my soul go to my mother and go inside of her. I traveled from this very place on a ray of light, all the way into my mother's womb. I saw myself being born from an observer's viewpoint as well as reliving the actual experience. I proceeded to see my entire life from the observer point of view as well as from the points of view of those my actions affected. I felt the feelings they felt that directly resulted from choices I made that affected them. I saw both the positive and the negative things I had done as they had truly happened; nothing of significance was left out or presented inaccurately.

I experienced the harshness of being born again. I experienced leaving what I felt to be heaven and the transit to Gaia. I saw myself as a helpless infant who needed his mother for everything. I experienced my father's love as well as his anger. I experienced my mother's love, her fear, and her anger as they applied to my being with her.

I saw all of the good and bad events from my childhood years and re-experienced the choices I made then. I was able to see everything significant that happened from all angles including the perspectives of the humans my choices affected. I felt all of my emotions and the emotions of the souls I had hurt as well as loved. Much of what I saw was surprising to me because there were more sides to the events than I was aware of when I was living my life. As I watched I thought to myself, I never realized, or I never knew. From all of this I learned that it matters deeply what choices I make while I am on Gaia.

I learned just how powerful we humans are and how we can affect each other in positive and negative ways, whether we think we are doing it or not. It was amazing to see how my innocent choices had such a powerful effect on souls that I had no idea I was affecting. The experience was one that I will never forget. I experienced the whole spectrum of feelings of my life in a relatively short period of time as we humans see it.

I could see how I became what I had become on Gaia and why I became that way. Everything I did in my life affected the evolution of the souls around me. I saw the reasons for all of my actions and understood why I did what I had done. There was a place for all of my positive and negative actions. There was no action that was necessarily wrong, but there were actions I took that didn't enhance positive growth in others.

It seemed that when I made choices that were purely for my own benefit, the resulting feelings of others were more likely to be of sadness, fear, or any other types of emotions that are less than loving and kind. I was both a victim and a beneficiary of every action I was shown, be it positive or negative. If the result of my actions from a global perspective were on the negative side, I was able to see the reasons for that and could see how I could have acted differently. From that, I learned what was not working to provide positive effect.

If I made choices that provided benefit to others without the expectation of a return from them, the resulting feelings were positive, loving, and kind. If the results of my choices were on the positive side, I would enjoy the feeling of them and know that if I continued to make similar choices, I would create more of that feeling. From that I learned what was working.

On the whole, this was not a fun experience for me to go through. I saw that many of my choices fostered negative effects. Actually, more were negative than positive. I didn't see how wonderful the review could have been if I had chosen to act to affect other souls positively most of the time.

One thing I wondered about was how the Council was able to show me my life. I guess they either monitored me, or my thought, word, and deed are written by me and stored someplace that they have access to.

Chapter 9: The Reckoning

After my records finished playing, the beings in the room asked me questions about what I saw and how I felt about my life up to then. I knew that I had to provide an honest assessment – I could not lie. I hesitated when they asked me whether I affected others more positively than negatively. I thought about lying to them and saying I affected others more positively, but I concluded that would not be the best thing for me to do because it was simply not true, if I did they would know anyway. I really liked where I was before the review started and really wanted to stay there. I had this idea that if I said "more positive", I would actually have more of a chance at staying.

I knew those beings knew what I was thinking and I had to tell them that I felt that I could have done a better job on Gaia. I knew why I had come to Gaia to accomplish. I was well on my way to doing that but now I knew I wasn't finished, yet I didn't want to leave the city and go back to Gaia. They agreed and told me that I still had many things to do and that I may want to go back and do them. I was told it was understood how difficult it would be for me but it was necessary for the universe for me to finish my path.

They said that it might be wise to go back and live my life how I had originally planned it. They said I had set lofty goals for my life on Gaia and the events in my life were achieving the goals I had set. They said that I originally came to Gaia to learn and share with others using the wisdom that I have accumulated over several lifetimes. They said that I am needed on Gaia to help souls bring themselves and Gaia back to harmony.

They said that I have great potential to affect other souls, to help them grow, and that Gaia is the best place to do that. I was told that the events I had experienced thus far were preparing me to make a large contribution to the universe and that my actions were not to be considered personal attacks in any way.

I didn't want to accept that. I wanted to stay and I expressed that feeling. I told them I was tired and wanted to stay because life on Gaia is hard and unforgiving. I even told them I felt that my return would be dangerous for the universe because I was not advanced enough in my spiritual evolution. They said that was precisely why it would be in my best interest to go back to Gaia. They said I was more advanced than I was willing to accept credit for and that I was shorting myself through not being proud of myself and not using the wonderful tools and potential that I carry with me in my heart and soul.

They said that it was possible for me to stay in the city but I would need to finish my work on Gaia sooner or later. The type of work I am destined for can only be done on Gaia. I could stay if I chose to but I would only be prolonging the completion of this phase of what I promised to do for this universe. They explained the fastest way to finish my work would be to go back to Gaia as soon as possible.

I was stunned to say the least. I became a bit angry as well. It was like I was given a present which was then promptly taken away. I resorted to bargaining with these beings but it was no use. I still didn't like the idea of living on Gaia and didn't really want to go back. These beings understood me but they remained firm. They would not bargain most likely because they were basing their advice on facts from my life review that calculated the same way every time and they were experts at it. I had a decision to make that was really the hardest decision I would ever make and I knew it.

I left the room with great reluctance. I was very sad that I couldn't remain in this great loving place. I was surprised that I could feel as well as choose sadness and anger here. Here I thought I was all done on Gaia and felt I was going to move on but I really was not quite ready yet. I was fearful of going back, especially because of the wisdom I was just given from this experience. I knew that Gaia could be a dangerous place for a soul. It is easy to backslide on Gaia. Temptations abound and choices are many. Choices are a great gift we have but they can be influenced so much by many things. If feelings from the heart are not followed, they can cause an overall negative effect on much more than anyone can possibly comprehend. Between what I had just learned and seeing my life over again, I respected the danger of staying as well as returning and felt my impending choice to be an extremely important one.

I met Bob outside. I told him what happened inside and he asked me what I was going to do. I told him I had to go back but I really didn't want to do that. I asked him if I could just stay with him and he told me the same things the beings inside told me. I told him that I had learned a great deal being with him and that I would be able to affect much if I were to stay with him and learned all that he could teach me. He told me to be patient. He agreed that I was accurate in what I said about learning so much from our interaction but I may want to weigh the decision in my heart before I decide.

I asked him if there was a way I could see ahead and use what I saw to assist me to decide.

He said that was permissible. Bob told me some of what would happen to me if I chose to return to Gaia. These were future things that would happen in my life. He told me that my life hardship would continue for many more years. He said I would have money problems and problems finding and keeping a job. I was to share my story. He said I would have this experience with me always and that I would face obstacles along the way that would keep me from sharing what I have learned.

Bob said that eventually people would seek me out so that I might help them answer their own questions about spirit. He said I would be a healer of souls and that I would assist other healers in the completion their paths. He said that I would marry and have several children. He explained the children I would create are extremely important to Gaia's future and part of my task is to nurture and protect them so that their paths would be more likely to be completed. My future children are part of my soul group. The group of us set goals that we were to help all of the individuals in the group. We planned it in the city of spirit together, and then came to Gaia at our appropriate time.

He said that my marriage would suffer and my family wouldn't be very happy until I learned my lessons on how to handle my energy in a positive way. He said once I learned to do that, I would then be evolved enough to begin to share my learning with many other souls.

I would be a big help in raising the energy of those souls as well. He said that it would be best if I shared this particular experience to all whom would choose to listen and believe and that I would learn yet more lessons from doing this. I was told that it would be a benefit to others for me to refrain from drugs and alcohol in order for me to exert more of my focus on serving others. Another reason I was given for refraining from substances was that if I used them my vibration would be limited greatly and I would also be prone to punishment from the authorities on Gaia. He said it was possible that I could lose my physical freedoms from being judged and thrown into jail for something related to this addiction. Bob also explained that I need to remain strong inside of myself and that the substances distort the feeling of confidence I would need to perform my tasks. Until I deemed myself worthy of my tasks, I would not be able to complete them.

Bob said that I would have some difficulty convincing myself as well as other humans that my experience was indeed real. He said I would eventually learn the best way and when to share the wisdom I was given and that I could only influence those who would choose to be influenced because it really is their decision. He told me that a friend of mine would die in a car accident. He said this friend would be drunk when this happened and I would contribute to this happening somehow. He explained to me that what I am to do in my future can be altered by me through the choices of which I am the master of - my own choices. I asked him when I was to return to be with him again. I wanted to know how and when I would be finished on Gaia in a physical form.

Bob said that I would be back after I had touched enough other souls and could answer the group of beings questions such as whether I thought I had affected those souls more positively than negatively with an answer that came with confidence from me, and without hesitation. He said I would eventually learn to reach for my confidence within and affect others in a positive way in this life, provided that I choose to positively grow my soul. He said if I made the choices in my life that truly came from my heart, after I was finished with this life that I would move on to complete a yet higher purpose in a form just like his. Trips to Gaia would become optional for me then. Bob then showed me to a garden where I could sit to think over my choices and make my decision.

Chapter 10: The Big Decision

    I went into that beautiful garden to make my decision. It was very peaceful and serene there. I was alone and had this really important decision to make. I assessed my options. It was amazing to me that I still had the free will to make the "wrong" decision, at least one that went against my true feelings. I suppose that even in the afterlife, choices still need to be made and like all choices the difficulty of them depends on the level of the evolution of a soul.

    I found myself thinking of the choices and feelings I knew were connected to the influences of all of my turns as a human. I thought about my role in the universe and the great gift of sight and feeling that I was given. I measured what the effect of a decision to stay, learn more, and then try again when I was ready would be. I thought of the vision I was given about the family I was to create as well the effect on other souls on Gaia should I return.

I thought of how wonderful Gaia is and how I saw firsthand what humans do to Gaia when they do not focus on being loving and kind with actions and thoughts that come from their hearts. I thought of the special persons I was to create and what the effect would be to the universe and Gaia if I instead chose to stay in this wonderful place and take the long way to complete my tasks.

The longer I thought, the more I realized that much of my thinking was based on a sort of self-centeredness. I was mostly contemplating how the decision was serving me. I was still looking for an excuse to not go back to Gaia. I was amazed that after everything I was shown so freely and with such love, I still could stay if I chose, but my choice could adversely affect the planet that I had fallen in love with all over again. Since the effect of me choosing to stay would benefit me mostly, I realized that by choosing to stay, I would not be making the choice out of love for the universe or for the souls in it. It would be only me who benefited, not be the universe.

I remembered that the being of light that guided me called me a master. I remembered the light of Master Jesus and what he told me. He didn't say for me to get as much I could by forgetting the feelings of other people. All he told me that was humans need to love one another. I thought about the service-oriented tone of my review and of the rest of my experience. I figured that to practice mastery, I would need to learn to be of service to others and to help others on their journeys in a manner that promotes harmony with all that is.

As I mulled over what I wanted to do, I realized what a master really is. It made sense to me to think that mastery is a level attained through growing one's soul enough so that the feelings that a soul carries can be shared with other souls to provide a service to them. This helps provide them what they might need to attain mastery themselves. This certainly made more sense to me than a master being the lord of the manor whose servants are expected to bow down in front of him through fear or intimidation. I understood that if I were really to be the master my friendly being said I was, I would need to take into account the feelings of others when I act. It occurred to me that a master is someone who lives to serve, and serves to live. A master is not someone whose main focus is to rule over others and make them do his

bidding for his or her own personal gain.
Examining everything from that perspective
helped me immensely to make my decision.

I decided to return to Gaia. After all, it was
the least I could do after receiving the great gift I
had been given. After all, time on Gaia isn't long
compared to forever. I felt that because of the gift
I received, I needed to make the service oriented
decision. After seeing what I saw and feeling
what I felt, for me to choose to stay in the city
would serve mostly me, so I decided to return to
Gaia to serve others.

I called for my sweet special being. He
appeared to me very quickly and I told him of my
decision. He was brimming with joy and told me
he was proud of me and that he would help me
when I needed help on Gaia. He told me that
even a being of his level has his assigned tasks
and that assisting me was one of his. He said that
his advancement depended in part on how
successful he was at influencing me to grow my
soul. He told me that I had helped him very much
through my decision. He said he always loved me
and found it remarkable that he could possibly
love me even more now! He told me that he
looked forward to the future that I originally
chose and am choosing yet again. He was so
excited!

He asked me when I was to return. I responded that although I loved this great place I was in, I felt a strong urgency to return to Gaia soon as possible to make the time I have to spend there go faster.

He then told me that one standard procedure for souls returning to Gaia was to drink water from the great river of life before they return. The water's purpose is to protect souls going back from knowing too much from their experience of the in between. The idea is for souls to experience Gaia in a natural way and evolve without potential distractions.

He said because I was chosen to carry my experience, I didn't have to drink the water before I came back. He said that I could drink if I chose to though. That was up to me. I didn't drink from the river because I felt that if I did, the peacefulness I was feeling would wash away along with the memories. My being did touch me on my lips to help me forget the things I could not share from my experience. The things I would forget would be those that if shared with the wrong people on Gaia would cause problems for them. I was to remember only the points I was shown that would be useful to me to complete this stage of my path and be effective in my service to others.

The being said that when I was ready, I could go back to Gaia and my purpose. Bob said I was to go back on my own. He said he would be in close contact with me and help guide me and protect me while it remained part of his purpose. I felt better about returning because I knew that my time on Gaia is minuscule in proportion to eternity. I knew that I would eventually return to that city later and that knowledge afforded me such great peace. I knew I would be OK if I went back to Gaia. I knew things would be hard for me but I felt that was OK because it was for the good of all, not just for my good. I remembered much wisdom that I didn't recall before the experience. I knew I would eventually be a great asset to the energies to humans, to Gaia, and the universe.

After that I began my return trip to Gaia and to my hometown. I followed the trail left from the connection to my physical body to find my way. I remember seeing the water tower at the Detroit Zoo as I neared home. The tower was a symbol that showed me that I was nearing the end of my trip back. It was fun to see my great mother Gaia alone, and without my Gaia-body. I could see the auras on everything and the sun was beginning to rise. I thought about checking out more places on Gaia prior to reuniting with my body but decided against it because I knew that it could be dangerous for me. I didn't want to chance being affected by the dark souls that I knew exist on Gaia and I didn't wish to delay my current physical life any longer. I felt my purpose was too important to chance being led away from the path I was to tread. I knew that I needed to be careful and that it may be best to move on and do what I needed to do instead of fooling around and getting in trouble.

I stopped at my home and checked on my sleeping family. I saw their auras and everything. I could see that they needed compassion and love from me. I wanted to see them before I got back in my body out of curiosity. I gave them some of my energy because I knew they needed it. I think my energy was what they really wanted from me all of my life anyway. I felt that I could give this energy to them freely and out of true love for them without letting them just take it from me. I realized that I really did love them and that they too are on the paths they need to be on and that I am a soul that is with them for good reason. I had learned much from them and they learned much from me. I realized that I had been withholding positive energy from them and that I needed to change that for the better.

After all, such as they were, they were still my family and are fellow souls just like me. I had been putting big conditions on my love for them and I knew that this was wrong. If I learned one thing from where I went, it was that true love is unconditional and placing conditions on it takes the true part away. If it were not for unconditional love, I would not have had the experience I had or learned what I learned!

I returned to my friend's house. Before I went inside, I took a moment to watch the sun rise. I have yet to experience another sunrise like that one. I could actually hear it rising and could see the energy coming toward the Earth. I felt this energy envelop my soul. That one sunrise inspired me greatly. I will never forget it. To me it symbolized a sort of rebirth and a promise for the future.

I felt that this dawning day was going to be very special because I had great wonders to share, work to do, and the energy to do both. I felt the sense of purpose that I had been searching for. I felt love in myself that I never really accepted or perhaps recognized before. I actually loved myself. I had allowed myself to become displaced from that feeling and it felt comforting to know that I could still feel that feeling of love for myself too. I felt peaceful and free and felt extremely confident I could make it here on Gaia. I could see this place with new eyes and with a new optimistic and positive outlook. I felt extremely blessed. I really looked forward to sharing what happened with the souls closest to me.

I went inside the house. I went inside easily because I thought myself inside. I had finally figured out that on Gaia I didn't need to touch things until I inhabited a body. I saw my friends sleeping in the family room of the house. There had to have been five or six teens passed out on the floor. I saw my body there, still lying in that chair just as I had left it. I didn't like to see it. After all the beauty I had seen, my body lying there without me inside it was not at all attractive to me. It seemed that without my soul my body had no purpose.

The "me" that was outside of my body was really the true me. I saw my body as merely the vehicle that the true "me" has to work with. I knew what would happen when I got back in my body and I didn't want to do it. I knew the freedom and the love the soul "me" felt would become lessened by the needed slowing of my vibration that enabled me to return to inhabit my body once again. I didn't wish to let the feelings I felt go away.

I did get back in my body though. I dare say that it was the hardest thing I have ever done. When I got back in, much of the love and peace I was feeling melted away. The freedom of movement was gone. I thought about going somewhere and couldn't go the same way I did without my body. I felt really heavy and slow. I awoke as soon as I rejoined my body and had much energy. I felt OK, except the energy I felt was not as intense as when I was out of my body. I remembered all of what happened to me and wanted to share my story right away while it was fresh in my mind.

Chapter 11: The After

After I had settled into my body, I got up and woke my friends to tell them what happened to me. I started to tell them the part about going to a place and waking up in the very distant past or the future. They just laughed at me and told me that I just overdosed on drugs and had a bad trip. They said I was crazy and to "stop my crazy talk." None of them understood what I was saying. They wouldn't listen and wanted no part of what I had to share whatsoever. I told them the being told me about mastery and my friend Jake said, "You are not MY master."

The guys were all tired from a long night of partying and I had just woken them up at the butt crack of dawn, babbling about this place I went to and what I am here to do. They said I just passed out in the chair all night because I overdosed on drugs and didn't go anywhere. They told me to just shut up about it. I told them that if the kind of trip I had was any indication, the drug I took could become very popular.

I readied myself to leave. I could not stay and continue to try to convince my friends of something they so obviously didn't want think of considering, much less believing. Not even one of them seemed to want to know anything about

82

what happened. I could see that the time was not right for what I had to share, at least for them.

I remember seeing my cigarettes on the bar and felt what was left of the bag of pot in my pocket. I rolled a joint for myself and had a cigarette as I rolled the joint. I made the decision to have a smoke and keep the pot because I figured I needed to use both of them to escape the all-too-familiar feeling of rejection once again. You see: I still had all of the problems here on Gaia that I had before the experience. I immediately felt that I still needed some sort of escape route, especially since I knew I was to have more of a tough life ahead of me.

I wondered how I could be of service to anyone if nobody was going to believe me. The initial reaction I received when I tried to share and the resulting loss of the feeling of peacefulness when I returned were key points in what I decided to do next. I decided that if my friends were not going to believe me and if the rest of my life was probably going to suck, I would just pretend the whole thing never happened. I regretted the decision I made to come back. For some reason I thought things would be magically different because I knew more about how the universe worked, but really it was me who was not ready to handle it. I needed to change. I felt the vibrations of my friends' thoughts as soon as I got back and felt that those thoughts were by no means positive. I felt a sense of danger pending if I stayed around them.

I went home and tried to sleep but couldn't for a long time. When I slept, the spirit I was with came to me in a dream. I couldn't see him but I heard his voice. He told me to find a psychic so I could learn how to use abilities I have been given. He said I would be able to see the futures of others. Bob told me a friend of mine would be killed drunk, driving a car. I thought about that and decided I didn't want to know anything or be a psychic. My stereotype of the psychic was that they were all broke and would take what they could gain from me for themselves. I'd rather work in the factories sweeping the floor. I told the spirit to leave me alone. I didn't want anyone to know about the voice because back then they locked people up for hearing voices.

You see, I wasn't a light being anymore. I was little Davey Oakford, the human with the life and level of development I had before the experience. I had the same thought patterns, the same sicknesses, and the same problems that got me to where I was. My vibration was just too low or out of control. There was no middle. I was still just 19 years old. My serious problems still needed to be addressed. I just couldn't handle another problem, which is what the experience was

84

beginning to be to me. I thought over what I experienced and listened to what my ego said about it. I worked on convincing myself that my friends were right. I was somewhat successful at it. I decided that if I was to be labeled as "crazy," it might be best for me to forget the whole thing ever happened or use what happened to make things easier for me personally, if anything.

Because of how my friends reacted to what I had to share, I could not even think about telling my family about this. My friends understood me better than anyone really and if they thought I was crazy, I was very sure my family would have me committed. I didn't trust my family to believe me because I still carried every bit of the mistrust of them I had before the experience. I felt all I would do is create more hurt than help if I told them.

A few months later I did try to remind my one friend several times that he needed to be careful with his drinking and driving but he chose to not listen to me. He even laughed at me about it, and then promptly told me to shut up about it and stop the "crazy talk." He didn't listen. He died that summer in a car crash while driving drunk, as advertised. The incident affected me greatly, enough to the point I considered myself one really messed up guy. Maybe I was crazy...maybe I still am? I didn't remember my experience more when that happened but ended up becoming angry with myself. I knew it was going to happen but lacked the communication skills and confidence to get an important warning message heard. I failed him. The last thing I ever wanted to think of then was my experience but I couldn't stop because I knew now that it had to be real. My friend's death and the circumstances surrounding it matched up.

I set out to continue my life. I knew that I would have employment problems and other problems so I set out to find work. The idea I had of my leaving the Detroit area fell by the wayside. I was very bitter about the whole deal. I set out to prove to the wonderful being that helped me as well as the entire group that showed me my life that they were wrong and I didn't need them or want them.

I still remembered what happened to me after I returned and one may think that after the experience that I would change my negative ways and focus on the positive. I did have good intent to do exactly that but chose to not do it for what I felt was a good reason.

You see: I came back here to Earth and immediately felt the negativity around where I was. It was the same negativity I was trying to get away from, and it was maybe even more of an influence than ever before. I let the negativity consume me once again because I didn't yet grow the skills necessary to avoid becoming influenced by it. It was very difficult for me to let go of my ego and the environmental influences around me to embrace something that really couldn't be substantially proven or otherwise be confirmed by another human.

I still didn't have the confidence within myself to take my feelings seriously, nor was I advanced enough to override the ego influences surrounding me. I also felt sad in my heart because I had gone to where I wanted to be, but chose to leave it all to help others that didn't seem to want my help.

I felt that there was nobody around with whom I could safely share what I was shown. I didn't feel safe writing this story afterward due to a fear in my heart that it would somehow be found and that I would be punished or disdained or called crazy for writing it or being told to shut up. I felt that I had these wonderful new clothes but no place or good reason to wear them. I felt lonelier than I felt before, more depressed than ever before, and I could see no avenue to express those feelings.

Chapter 12: Today

Here I sit, decades later. Life for me came off the same way I understood it would. I did get married. I did have employment, money, and marriage problems and all of them happened the way they were supposed to happen, despite my attempts to change them to what I thought was my liking. This life has for certain been a growing experience for me. I eventually overcame my depression and grew the confidence to share this story, but it sure took a long time. During that time a lot of darkness occurred over my life's path. I do understand though that it has been time well spent, and I appreciate the hard trials I have had in my life. I feel I am stronger for having them and I accept them.

The universe has provided me with reminders of the experience over the years. I remember reading Betty J. Eadie's "Embraced By the Light" in 1992. Reading her story provided me confirmation that what happened to me in 1979 was indeed for real and very special. It helped give me the confidence to tell my story to others then. It inspired me to begin to live my life according to the insights I learned from my experience. I appreciate Mrs. Eadie for sharing her experience and touching the many souls I know she has touched.

The next reminder the universe left for me was a book called "The Celestine Prophecy" by James Redfield. As soon as I began to read it, the metaphysical concepts presented in the book persuaded me to evaluate myself from the viewpoint of what I was doing with my energies. It even had information about auras and how they work. The book confirmed many of the insights my experience contained concerning the interaction of energies between humans. It prompted me to explore more in the metaphysical areas of bookstores. I discovered a host of published works that provided even more confirmation about other insights presented to me long ago. Eventually, the more I explored, the more I felt an urge to share my story with others. Eventually I began frequenting the AOL Metaphysics chat-rooms. From those humble beginnings, "Soul Bared" came about.

I see the worldwide web as an extremely valuable tool to learn about concepts metaphysical in nature and anything else one might care to learn about. Use Google, ask questions. I'm not a scholar of metaphysics by any means, but I do offer that the web does provide a wealth of information that rings true to me. It probably has much more information on spiritual matters that I can possibly learn in one life. Books are another way to learn more, as they always have been. It's not a bad deal to go retro. I'm reasonably sure that what I have learned from the experience is most likely already recorded somewhere (in my soul record) and I take great delight when I see something I find that rings true to me.

I feel that my heart is fully capable of determining whether or not I should believe what I read. I also know that the universe will guide me to what I need to know, naturally, provided I make a conscious effort to follow my intuition and transmit and receive positive vibration.

I really dislike saying that I went on this wonderful trip and only brought back the simple message of loving one another, but I have to call it as I see it. I feel that one simple philosophy has great merit and is the master key to all that is. It really isn't hard to do. I think about this world today and see the immense impact that even one seemingly tiny decision to send someone a kind thought or smile or deed can make. Everyone can smile.

If an incentive to be loving and kind to others is really needed, it is nice know that each act of kindness is recorded and will eventually be re-experienced much later on. It doesn't matter if the act is one that promotes a smile from one person to another or if it is one country helping another to live in harmony with the planet. To me, the concept is the same really and all of it counts the same. Sure, one can always decide to harness the opposite of being loving and kind due to free will and all, but the universe has rules regulating the outcome of that choice, rules which I feel make sense. One of the rules is that as positive as positive gets, negative reciprocates in kind. I see the justice in that principle and feel comfortable knowing that type of structure exists in the universe itself.

For me, the choice for either positive or negative is always present. I feel one of the greatest gifts given to humans is choice. The day I remembered that I do have a choice about what I wish to contribute to the planet and humanity was one of my favorite days in this particular lifetime on this planet! It signaled a new beginning of a shift in thought for me, one that focused on using my feelings with the intent of promoting positive vibration on the planet.

I have been reflecting on what happened to me and have been trying to make sense of it all. I feel that the main focus of the whole experience concerns how I interact with other humans and with Gaia. I learned in my experience that Gaia is a living, breathing being. We need to give her a break and stop ruining her. She has feelings. Because she is strong, she adjusts herself when she needs to and might just fight back. I know every thought and deed I choose affects her. If I am negative, the negativity manifests itself in her just as easily as it would if I subjected another human to the same negativity. I know positive thoughts and deeds work the same way.

I know I'm not perfect. I understand there will be times when I will contribute negative vibration to the universe in the course of my learning. I feel Jesus and any other of the great masters would be OK with it so long as I balance it with positive. I know they understand how all of my choices help my soul grow. The masters are smart.   A goal I strive to reach is to learn what I need to learn and make sure I clean up any messes I might make in the course of my growth and development. Hopefully, I will contribute more positive than negative, or at least try to travel the middle road.

I'm glad to have had the opportunity to place my story out in the open because I feel better about it now. It's my hope that those who have read this story take with them something they can use in their lives, something that will inspire them to love one another and make positive vibration. We can do this. We have to.